BOB

BOB

SIDNEY LANIER

ISBN: 978-93-5614-514-6

Published: 1910

LECTOR HOUSE LLP
E-MAIL: lectorpublishing@gmail.com

BOB
THE STORY OF OUR MOCKING-BIRD

BY

SIDNEY LANIER

WITH SIXTEEN ILLUSTRATIONS IN COLOR

1910

PREFATORY NOTE

The poet Sidney Lanier loved to swing in full-muscled walks through the fields and woods; to take the biggest bow and quiver out of the archery implements provided for himself and his brood of boys, and with them trailing at his heels, to tramp and shoot at rovers; to bestride a springy horse and ride through the mountains and the valleys, noting what they were pleased to show of tree and bird and beast life. He could feel the honest savage instinct of the hunter (and lose it in his first sight of a stag's death-eyes). A rare bird's nest with eggs produced in him the rapture vouchsafed to barbarian Boy, along with the divine suggestions vouchsafed to the Poet. This may be worth while to say to those of Lanier's readers who may think of him as a sensitive, delicate man of letters, and who must see in most of his writing evidences of extreme sensibility. It was this habit of a practical, face-to-face conversation with nature which, joined with the artist's instinct, makes the sketch of "Bob" so veracious a picture of a bird-individual and a bird-species. Lanier's wife and children remember well the delight the bird had for his brother artist; how the amused flute would trill with extravagant graces to the silent but heedful wonder of the caged one. Every surprising token of intelligence, of affection, of valor displayed by Bob was hailed by Mr. Lanier with a boy's ecstacy over a pet, and a poet's thankfulness of a beautiful work of the Creator.

There is, doubtless, no need to assure the reader that the events of Bob's life as hereinafter depicted are historically true; he was acquired by one of the poet's boys, who, forbidden to rob nests, remembers his fear, on the way home with Bob in his straw hat, that the account of the bird's helpless condition would not serve as a fair and reasonable excuse for keeping him as a pet.

The illustrations which form so important a part of the effort to make a picture of Bob, are unusual in their origin and in their method. Mr. Dugmore made photographic studies of a young mocking-bird, or, rather, of a number of young mocking-birds, the photographs were colored by him, and the plates from these photographs were printed in color. The variety of rare tints in any bird's plumage, their extreme delicacy, and the infinitely fine gradations of shading have almost always baffled the artist and the printer. The present attempt to reproduce Mr. Dugmore's masterly pictures in color shows at least a handsome advance in the difficult art.

CHARLES DAY LANIER.

October, 1899.

LIST OF ILLUSTRATIONS

From Photographs made from Life and colored by A. R. Dugmore

THE MOCKING-BIRD

Superb and sole, upon a pluméd spray
That o'er the general leafage boldly grew,
He summ'd the woods in song; or typic drew
The watch of hungry hawks, the lone dismay,
Of languid doves when long their lovers stray,
And all birds' passion-plays that sprinkle dew
At morn in brake or bosky avenue.
Whate'er birds did or dreamed, this bird could say.
Then down he shot, bounced airily along
The sward, twitched in a grasshopper, made song
Midflight, perched, prinked, and to his art again.
Sweet Science, this large riddle read me plain:
How may the death of that dull insect be
The life of yon trim Shakspere on the tree?

BOB

Not that his name *ought* to be Bob at all. In respect of his behavior during a certain trying period which I am presently to recount, he ought to be called Sir Philip Sidney: yet, by virtue of his conduct in another very troublesome business which I will relate, he has equal claim to be known as Don Quixote de la Mancha: while, in consideration that he is the Voice of his whole race, singing the passions of all his fellows better than any one could sing his own, he is clearly entitled to be named William Shakspere.

For Bob is our mocking-bird. He fell to us out of the top of a certain great pine in a certain small city on the sea-coast of Georgia. In this tree and a host of his lordly fellows which tower over that little city, the mocking-birds abound in unusual numbers. They love the prodigious masses of the leaves, and the generous breezes from the neighboring Gulf Stream, and, most of all, the infinite flood of the sunlight which is so rich and cordial that it will make even a man lift his head towards the sky, as a mocking-bird lifts his beak, and try to sing something or other.

About three years ago, in a sandy road which skirts a grove of such tall pines, a wayfarer found Bob lying in a lump. It could not have been more than a few days since he was no bird at all, only an egg with possibilities. The finder brought him to our fence and turned him over to a young man who had done us the honor to come out of a Strange Country and live at our house about six years before. Gladly received by this last, Bob was brought within, and family discussions were held. He could not be put back into a tree: the hawks would have had him in an hour. The original nest was not to be found. We struggled hard against committing the crime—as we had always considered it—of caging a bird. But finally it became plain that there was no other resource. In fact, we were obliged to recognize that he had come to us from the hand of Providence, and, though we are among the most steady-going democrats of this Republic, we were yet sufficiently acquainted with the etiquette of courts to know that one does not refuse the gift of the King.

Dimly hoping, therefore, that we might see our way clear to devise some means of giving Bob an education that would fit him for a forester, we arranged suitable accommodations for him, and he was tended with motherly care.

He repaid our attentions from the very beginning. He immediately began to pick up in flesh and to increase the volume of his rudimentary feathers. Soon he commenced to call for his food as lustily as any spoiled child. When it was brought, he would throw his head back and open his yellow-lined beak to a width which no one would credit who did not see it. Into this enormous cavity, which seemed almost larger than the bird, his protectress would thrust—and the more vigorously the better he seemed to like it—ball after ball of the yolk of hard-boiled egg mashed up with Irish potato.

"Bob lying in a lump"

"To increase the volume of his rudimentary feathers"

How, from this dry compound which was his only fare except an occasional worm off the rose-bushes, Bob could have wrought the surprising nobleness of spirit which he displayed about six weeks after he came to us ... is a matter which I do not believe the most expansive application of Mr. Herbert Spencer's theory of the genesis of emotion could even remotely account for. I refer to the occasion when he fairly earned the title of Sir Philip Sidney. A short time after he became our guest a couple of other fledgelings were brought and placed in his cage. One of these soon died, but the other continued for some time longer to drag out a drooping existence. One day, when Bob was about six weeks old, his usual ration had been delayed, owing to the pressure of other duties upon his attendant. He was not slow to make this circumstance known by all the language available to him. He was very hungry indeed and was squealing with every appearance of entreaty and of indignation when at last the lady of the house was able to bring him his breakfast. He scrambled to the bars of the cage—which his feeble companion was unable to do—took the proffered ball of egg-and-potato fiercely in his beak, and then, instead of swallowing it, deliberately flapped back to his sick guest in the corner and gave him the whole of it without tasting a morsel.

"Throw his head back and open his yellow-lined beak"

"He scrambled to the bars of the cage — which his feeble companion was unable to do"

Now when Sir Philip Sidney was being carried off the battle-field of Zutphen with a fearful wound in his thigh, he became very thirsty and begged for water. As the cup was handed him, a dying soldier who lay near cast upon it a look of great longing. This Sidney observed: refusing the cup, he ordered that it should be handed to the soldier, saying, "His necessity is greater than mine."

 mocking-bird is called Bob just as a goat is called Billy or Nan, as a parrot is called Poll, as a squirrel is called Bunny, or as a cat is called Pussy or Tom. In spite of the suggestions forced upon us by the similarity of his behavior to that of the sweet young gentleman of Zutphen, our bird continued to bear the common appellation of his race and no efforts on the part of those who believe in the fitness of things have availed to change the habits of Bob's friends in this particular. Bob he was, is, and will probably remain.

Perhaps under a weightier title he would not have thriven so prosperously. His growth was amazing in body and in mind. By the time he was two months old he clearly showed that he was going to be a singer. About this period certain little feeble trills and experimental whistles began to vary the monotony of his absurd squeals and chirrups. The musical business, and the marvellous work of feathering himself, occupied his thoughts continually. I cannot but suppose that he superintended the disposition of the black, white and gray markings on his wings and his tail as they successively appeared: he certainly manufactured the pigments with which those colors were laid on, somewhere within himself,—and all out of egg-and-potato. How he ever got the idea of arranging his feather characteristics exactly as those of all other male mocking-birds are arranged—is more than I know. It is equally beyond me to conceive why he did not—while he was about it—exert his individuality to the extent of some little peculiar black dot or white stripe whereby he could at least tell himself from any other bird. His failure to attend to this last matter was afterwards the cause of a great battle from which Bob would have emerged in a plight as ludicrous as any of Don Quixote's,—considering the harmless and unsubstantial nature of his antagonist—had not this view of his behavior been changed by the courage and spirit with which he engaged his enemy, the gallantry with which he continued the fight, and the good faithful blood which he shed while it lasted. In all these particulars his battle fairly rivalled any encounter of the much-bruised Knight of la Mancha.

He was about a year old when it happened, and the fight took place a long way from his native heath. He was spending the summer at a pleasant country home in Pennsylvania. He had appeared to take just as much delight in the clover fields and mansion-studded hills of this lovely region as in the lonesome forests and sandy levels of his native land. He had sung, and sung: even in his dreams at night his sensitive little soul would often get quite too full and he would pour forth rapturous bursts of sentiment at any time between twelve o'clock and daybreak. If our health had been as little troubled by broken slumber as was his, these melodies in the late night would have been glorious; but there were some of us who had gone into the country especially to sleep; and we were finally driven to swing the sturdy songster high up in our outside porch at night, by an apparatus contrived with careful reference to cats. Several of these animals in the neighborhood had longed unspeakably for Bob ever since his arrival. We had seen them eyeing him from behind bushes and through windows, and had once rescued him from one who had thrust a paw between the very bars of his cage. That cat was going to eat him, art and all, with no compunction in the world. His music seemed to make no more impression on cats than Keats's made on critics. If only some really discriminating person had been by with a shot-gun when *The Quarterly* thrust its paw into poor Endymion's cage!

"For it was his own image in the looking-glass of a bureau"

"His bath"

"When he smoothed his feathers"

One day at this country-house Bob had been let out of his cage and allowed to fly about the room. He had cut many antics, to the amusement of the company, when presently we left him, to go down to dinner. What occurred afterward was very plainly told by circumstantial evidence when we returned. As soon as he was alone, he had availed himself of his unusual freedom to go exploring about the room. In the course of his investigation he suddenly found himself confronted by ... it is impossible to say what he considered it. If he had been reared in the woods he would probably have regarded it as another mocking-bird, — for it was his own image in the looking-glass of a bureau. But he had never seen any member of his race except the forlorn little unfledged specimen which he had fed at six weeks of age, and which bore no resemblance to this tall, gallant, bright-eyed figure in the mirror. He had thus had no opportunity to generalize his kind; and he knew nothing whatever of his own personal appearance except the partial hints he may have gained when he smoothed his feathers with his beak after his bath in the morning. It may therefore very well be that he took this sudden apparition for some Chimæra or dire monster which had taken advantage of the family's temporary absence to enter the room, with evil purpose. Bob immediately determined to defend the premises. He flew at the invader, literally beak and claw. But beak and claw taking no hold upon the smooth glass, with each attack he slid struggling down to the foot of the mirror. Now it so happened that a pin-cushion lay at this point, which bristled not only with pins but with needles which had been temporarily left in it and which were nearly as sharp at the eye-ends as at the points. Upon these Bob's poor claws came down with fury: he felt the wounds and saw the blood: both he attributed to the strokes of his enemy, and this roused him to new rage. In order to give additional momentum to his onset he would retire towards the other side of the room and thence fly at the foe. Again and again he charged: and as many times slid down the smooth surface of the mirror and wounded himself upon the perilous pin-cushion. As I entered, being first up from table, he was in the act of fluttering down against the glass. The counterpane on the bed, the white dimity cover of the bureau, the pin-cushion, all bore the bloody resemblances of his feet in various places, and showed how many times he had sought distant points in order to give himself a running start. His heart was beating violently, and his feathers were ludicrously tousled. And all against the mere shadow of himself! Never was there such a temptation for the head of a family to assemble his people and draw a prodigious moral. But better thoughts came: for, after all, was it not probable that the poor bird was defending — or at any rate believed he was defending — the rights and properties of his absent masters against a foe of unknown power? All the circumstances go to show that he made the attack with a faithful valor as reverent as that which steadied the lance of Don Quixote against the windmills. In after days, when his cage has been placed among the boughs of the trees, he has not shown any warlike feelings against the robins and sparrows that passed about, but only a friendly interest.

"And as many times slid down the smooth surface of the mirror and wounded himself upon the perilous pin-cushion"

"The most elegant, trim ... little dandy"

At this present writing, Bob is the most elegant, trim, electric, persuasive, cunning, tender, courageous, artistic little dandy of a bird that mind can imagine. He does not confine himself to imitating the songs of his tribe. He is a creative artist. I was witness not long ago to the selection and adoption by him of a rudimentary whistle-language. During an illness it fell to my lot to sleep in a room alone with Bob. In the early morning, when a lady—to whom Bob is passionately attached—would make her appearance in the room, he would salute her with a certain joyful chirrup which appears to belong to him peculiarly. I have not heard it from any other bird. But sometimes the lady would merely open the door, make an inquiry, and then retire. It was now necessary for his artistic soul to find some form of expressing grief. For this purpose he selected a certain cry almost identical with that of the cow-bird—an indescribably plaintive, long-drawn, thin whistle. Day after day I heard him make use of these expressions. He had never done so before. The mournful one he would usually accompany, as soon as the door was shut, with a sidelong, inquiring posture of the head, which was a clear repetition of the lover's *Is she gone? Is she really gone?*

"A sidelong, inquiring posture of the head, ... Is she gone?"

here is one particular in which Bob's habits cannot be recommended. He eats very often. In fact if Bob should hire a cook, it would be absolutely necessary for him to write down his hours for her guidance; and this writing would look very much like a time-table of the Pennsylvania, or the Hudson River, or the Old Colony, Railroad. He would have to say: "Bridget will be kind enough to get me my breakfast at the following hours: 5, 5.30, 5.40, 6, 6.15, 6.30, 6.45, 7, 7.20, 7.40, 8 (and so on, every fifteen or twenty minutes, until 12 M.); my dinner at 12, 12.20, 12.40, 1, 1.15, 1.30 (and so on every fifteen or twenty minutes until 6 p.m.); my supper is irregular, but I wish Bridget particularly to remember that I *always* eat whenever I awake in the night, and that I usually awake four or five times between bedtime and daybreak." With all this eating, Bob never neglects to wipe his beak after each meal. This he does by drawing it quickly, three or four times on each side, against his perch.

"He eats very often"

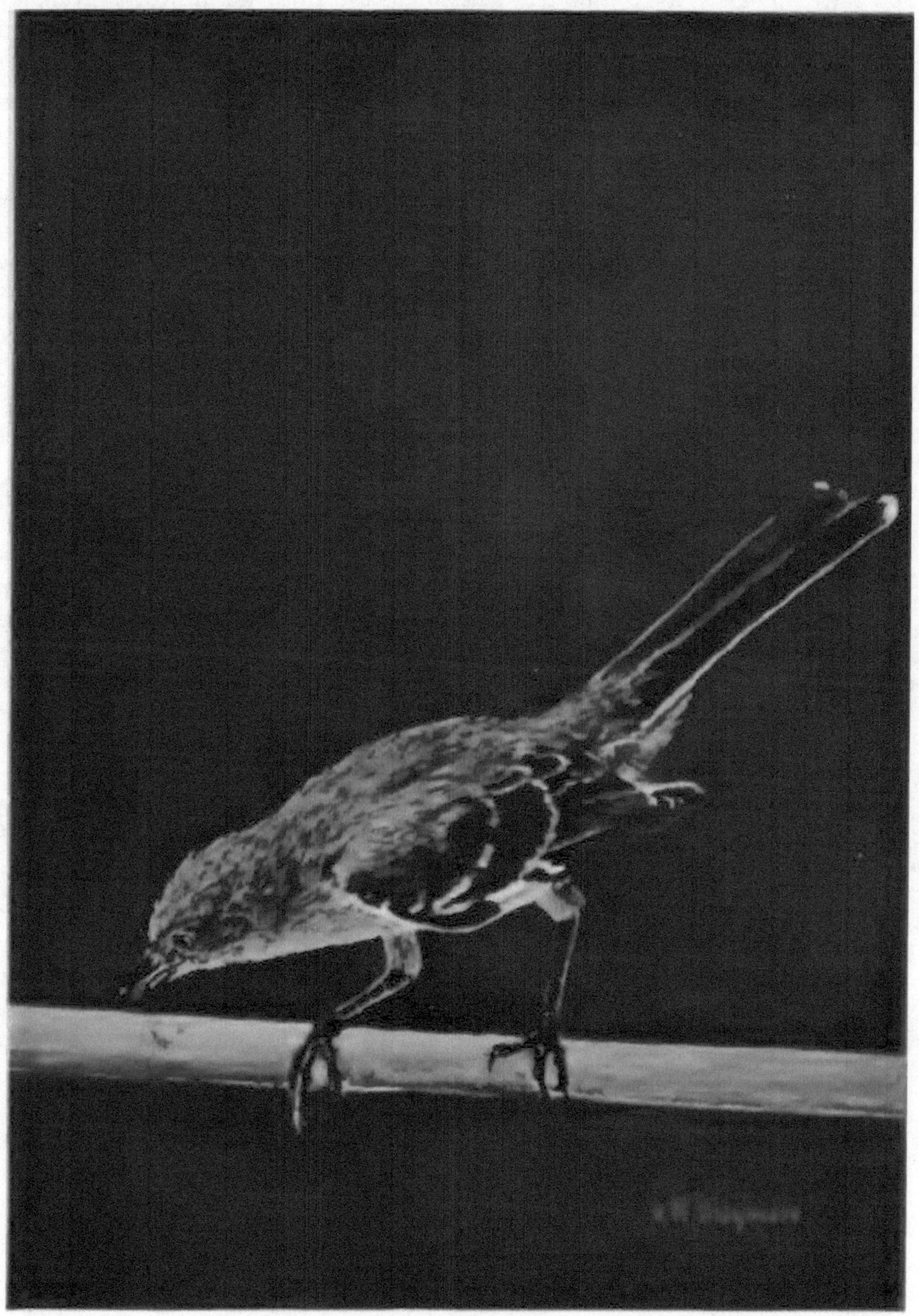

"Bob never neglects to wipe his beak after each meal"

I never tire of watching his motions. There does not seem to be the least friction between any of the component parts of his system. They all work, give, play in and out, stretch, contract, and serve his desires generally with a smoothness and soft precision truly admirable.

Merely to see him leap from his perch to the floor of his cage is to me a never-failing marvel. It is so instantaneous, and yet so quiet: *clip,* and he is down, with his head in the food-cup: I can compare it to nothing but the stroke of Fate. It is perhaps a strained association of the large with the small: but when he suddenly leaps down in this instantaneous way, I always feel as if, while looking down upon the three large Forms of the antique Sculpture, lying in severe postures along the ground, I suddenly heard the clip of the fatal shears.

His repertory of songs is extensive. Perhaps it would have been much more so if his life had been in the woods where he would have had the opportunity to hear the endlessly-various calls of his race. So far as we can see, the stock of songs which he now sings must have been brought in his own mind from the egg, or from some further source whereof we know nothing. He certainly never *learned* these calls: many of the birds of whom he gives perfect imitations have been always beyond his reach. He does not apprehend readily a new set of tones. He has caught two or three musical phrases from having them whistled near him. No systematic attempt, however, has been made to teach him anything. His procedure in learning these few tones was peculiar. He would not, on first hearing them, make any sign that he desired to retain them, beyond a certain air of attention in his posture. Upon repetition on a different day, his behavior was the same: there was no *attempt* at imitation. But sometime afterward, quite unexpectedly, in the hilarious flow of his birdsongs would appear a perfect reproduction of the whistled tones. Like a great artist he was rather above futile and amateurish efforts. He took things into his mind, turned them over, and, when he was perfectly sure of them, brought them forth with perfection and with unconcern.

He has his little joke. His favorite response to the endearing terms of the lady whom he loves is to scold her. Of course he understands that she understands his wit. He uses for this purpose the angry warning cry which mocking-birds are in the habit of employing to drive away intruders from their nests. At the same time he expresses his delight by a peculiar gesture which he always uses when pleased. He extends his right wing and stretches his leg along the inner surface of it as far as he is able.

He has great capacities in the way of elongating and contracting himself. When he is curious, or alarmed, he stretches his body until he seems incredibly tall and of the size of his neck all the way. When he is cold, he makes himself into a round ball of feathers.

"He stretches his body until he seems incredibly tall"

"When he is cold, he makes himself into a round ball of feathers"

think I envy him most when he goes to sleep. He takes up one leg somewhere into his bosom, crooks the other a trifle, shortens his neck, closes his eyes,—and it is done. He does not appear to hover a moment in the borderland between sleeping and waking but hops over the line with the same superb decision with which he drops from his perch to the floor. I do not think he ever has anything on his mind after he closes his eyes. It is my belief that he never committed a sin of any sort in his whole life. There is but one time when he ever looks sad. This is during the season when his feathers fall. He is then unspeakably dejected. Never a note do we get from him until it is over. Nor can he be blamed. Last summer not only the usual loss took place, but every feather dropped from his tail. His dejection during this period was so extreme that we could not but believe he had some idea of his personal appearance under the disadvantage of no tail. This was so ludicrous that his most ardent lovers could scarcely behold him without a smile; and it appeared to cut him to the soul that he should excite such sentiments.

"When his feathers fall. He is then unspeakably dejected.... every feather dropped from his tail"

"We have only to set Bob's cage where a spot of sunshine will fall on it....
up goes his beak, and he is off"

But in a surprisingly short time his tail-feathers grew out again, the rest of his apparel reappeared fresh and new, and he lifted up his head: insomuch that whenever we wish to fill the house with a gay, confident, dashing, riotous, innocent, sparkling glory of jubilation, we have only to set Bob's cage where a spot of sunshine will fall on it. His beads of eyes glisten, his form grows intense, up goes his beak, and he is off.

Finally we have sometimes discussed the question: is it better on the whole, that Bob should have lived in a cage than in the wildwood? There are conflicting opinions about it: but one of us is clear that it is. He argues that although there are many songs which are never heard, as there are many eggs which never hatch, yet the general end of a song is to be heard, as that of an egg is to be hatched. He further argues that Bob's life in his cage has been one long blessing to several people who stood in need of him: whereas in the woods, leaving aside the probability of hawks and bad boys, he would not have been likely to gain one appreciative listener for a single half-hour out of each year. And, as I have already mercifully released you from several morals (continues this disputant) which I might have drawn from Bob, I am resolved that no power on earth shall prevent me from drawing this final one. — We have heard much of "the privileges of genius," of "the right of the artist to live out his own existence free from the conventionalities of society," of "the un-morality of art," and the like. But I do protest that the greater the artist, and the more profound his pity toward the fellow-man for whom he passionately works, the readier will be his willingness to forego the privileges of genius and to cage himself in the conventionalities, even as the mocking-bird is caged. His struggle against these will, I admit, be the greatest: he will feel the bitterest sense of their uselessness in restraining *him* from wrong-doing. But, nevertheless, one consideration will drive him to enter the door and get contentedly on his perch: his fellow-men, his fellow-men. These he can reach through the respectable bars of use and wont; in his wild thickets of lawlessness they would never hear him, or, hearing, would never listen. In truth this is the sublimest of self-denials, and none but a very great artist can compass it: to abandon the sweet green forest of liberty, and live a whole life behind needless constraints, for the more perfect service of his fellow-men.

EPILOGUE

TO OUR MOCKING-BIRD

DIED OF A CAT, MAY, 1878

I

Trillets of humor,—shrewdest whistle-wit,—
Contralto cadences of grave desire
Such as from off the passionate Indian pyre
Drift down through sandal-odored flames that split
About the slim young widow who doth sit
And sing above,—midnights of tone entire,—
Tissues of moonlight shot with songs of fire;—
Bright drops of tune, from oceans infinite
Of melody, sipped off the thin-edged wave
And trickling down the beak,—discourses brave
Of serious matter that no man may guess,—
Good-fellow greetings, cries of light distress—
All these but now within the house we heard:
O Death, wast thou too deaf to hear the bird?

II

Ah me, though never an ear for song, thou hast
A tireless tooth for songsters: thus of late
Thou camest, Death, thou Cat! and leap'st my gate,
And, long ere Love could follow, thou hadst passed
Within and snatched away, how fast, how fast,
My bird—wit, songs, and all—thy richest freight
Since that fell time when in some wink of fate
Thy yellow claws unsheathed and stretched, and cast
Sharp hold on Keats, and dragged him slow away,
And harried him with hope and horrid play—
Ay, him, the world's best wood-bird, wise with song—
Till thou hadst wrought thine own last mortal wrong.
'Twas wrong! 'twas wrong! I care not, *wrong's* the word—
To munch our Keats and crunch our mocking-bird.

III

Nay, Bird; my grief gainsays the Lord's best right.
The Lord was fain, at some late festal time,
That Keats should set all Heaven's woods in rhyme,
And thou in bird-notes. Lo, this tearful night,
Methinks I see thee, fresh from death's despite,
Perched in a palm-grove, wild with pantomime,
O'er blissful companies couched in shady thyme,
—Methinks I hear thy silver whistlings bright
Mix with the mighty discourse of the wise,
Till broad Beethoven, deaf no more, and Keats,
'Midst of much talk, uplift their smiling eyes,
And mark the music of thy wood-conceits,
And halfway pause on some large, courteous word,
And call thee "Brother," O thou heavenly Bird!

Baltimore, 1878.

Lector House believes that a society develops through a two-fold approach of continuous learning and adaptation, which is derived from the study of classic literary works spread across the historic timeline of literature records. Therefore, we aim at reviving, repairing and redeveloping all those inaccessible or damaged but historically as well as culturally important literature across subjects so that the future generations may have an opportunity to study and learn from past works to embark upon a journey of creating a better future.

This book is a result of an effort made by Lector House towards making a contribution to the preservation and repair of original ancient works which might hold historical significance to the approach of continuous learning across subjects.

HAPPY READING & LEARNING!

LECTOR HOUSE LLP
E-MAIL: lectorpublishing@gmail.com